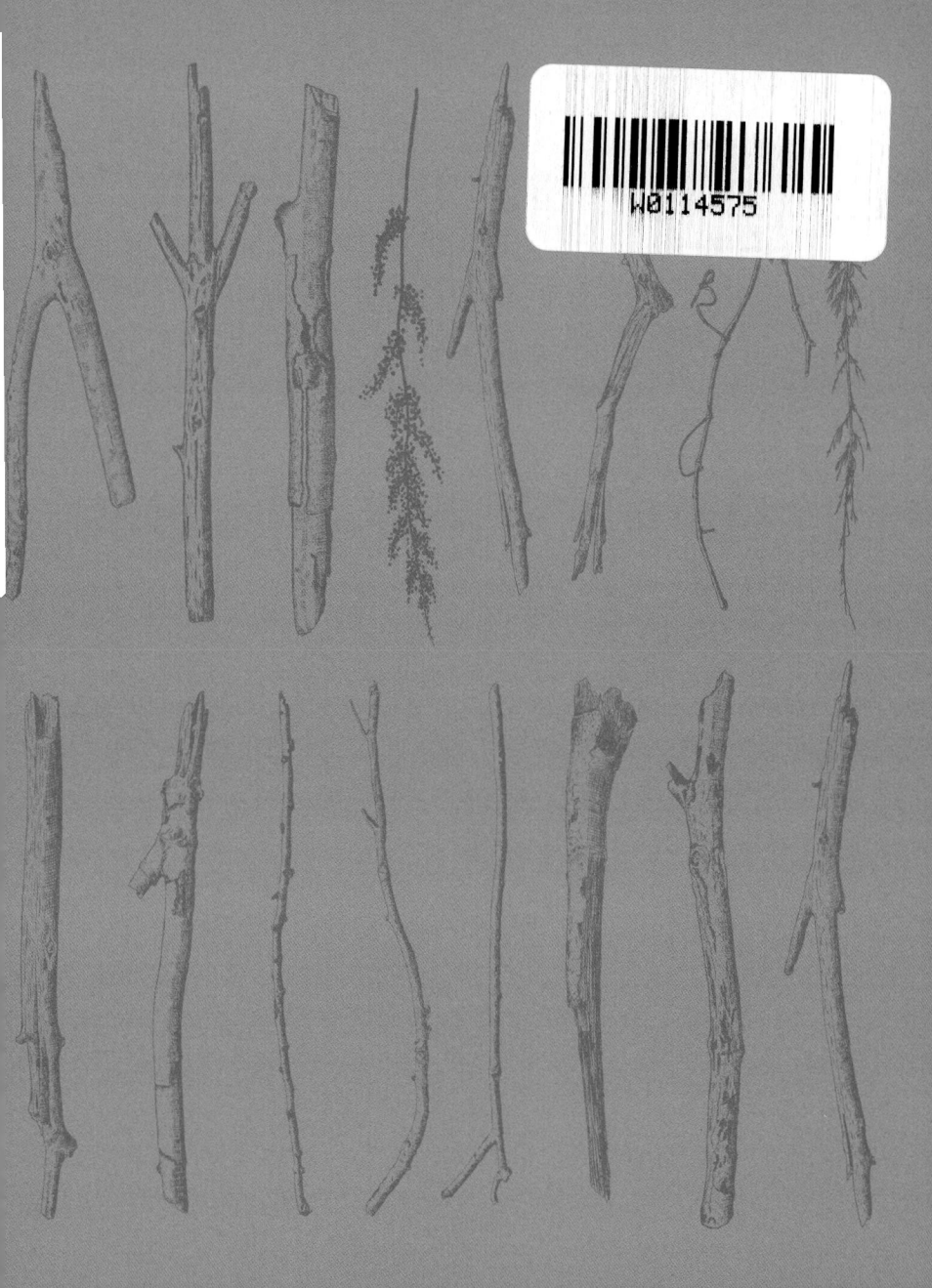

STICKS

A COLLECTION OF STICKS & THE PEOPLE WHO LOVE THEM, FROM THE FOUNDERS OF STICK NATION

LOGAN JUGLER & BOONE HOGG

TEN SPEED PRESS
California | New York

CONTENTS

INTRODUCTION

Hi! We're Boone Hogg and Logan Jugler. And we like sticks.
Maybe you haven't realized it, but we're guessing you like sticks, too.

Think about it. Pretty much everyone has picked up a stick on a walk or a hike or in a backyard and imagined it was something more. Remember in childhood, how a stick became a monster-defeating sword or a sorcerer's magic wand? Even for an adult, a stick can quickly become a functional cane or a walking stick. And if you're a dog, a stick is pure joy.

A stick can also be a meaningful reminder of a person, a place, a trip, or a moment in time. Every stick has a different aura, a different shape, color, and texture. They can make you feel powerful, playful, or small.

One summer, while on a hiking trip with friends in Utah's Arches National Park, we picked up a stick from the side of the trail—a small one, smooth and sturdy, with a nice slight bend—and started debating if it was a good stick.

We liked the shape of the stick. It had a really nice curvature. A solid color, nice grains, felt good in the hand. A lot to love about the stick.

We jokingly debated amongst our small group of friends: "What makes a good stick?" We rated this stick a middling 5 out of 10.

After returning home, on a whim we posted a video of our stick review on our new social media account, @officialstickreviews. To our surprise, we learned we weren't the only people who really love sticks. As we started posting more videos of our stick reviews, people started to send *us* their stick treasures and stick reviews. It was unbelievable! What started as a silly conversation between friends quickly turned into a global phenomenon. We've gotten tens of thousands of submissions from more than a hundred countries around the world.

A man from France sent in a dinosaur-shaped stick from his recently deceased father's stick collection.

A couple sent in a hiking stick that helped them traverse to the peak of Mount Rinjani in Indonesia.

What draws people to sticks? Why are they so widely beloved?

Sticks are simple. They're universal. They've been around forever. No matter our location, our interests, or our political beliefs, sticks are a language we all speak.

In a world dominated by technology and rapid change, sticks are a reminder of the power of imagination. They're a blank slate for wonder and creativity. Sticks encourage us to pause and reconnect with nature.

Throughout the pages of this book, we'll share with you the basics of stick reviewing, encouraging you to get outside, explore, and find sticks. You'll find photos and anecdotes submitted to us from stick lovers around the world (and of course, feel free to rate each on your own!).

But most of all, we hope you'll rediscover the joy of being a kid, the outdoors, and the simple beauty of being human.

This is our love letter to everyone who understands the happiness and triumph of finding a good stick.

Welcome to Stick Nation.

STICKTIONARY

Now that your attention has been turned to sticks—the ones you stumble upon in the woods, go on missions to collect, already have piled in your garage, or simply see in a photo or video—you might want to start reviewing them yourself. When you first begin reviewing sticks, you may find yourself wondering, *What are the classes of sticks? What determines the quality of a stick?* Don't worry. We've got you. Read on!

> The burning question: What *is* a stick? Is a log a stick? Is a branch a stick? At what point does a piece of wood become a stick—or stop being one?
>
> Technically, a stick is defined as a piece of wood that grew from and was once attached to a tree. But, to us, a stick is much more than that. A stick stirs up imagination. A stick brings joy.

Here is a brief overview of stick classes, traits, and attributes that will help you as you enter the world of stick reviewing.

STICK CLASSES

One of the first steps of your stick reviewing journey is to understand the different characteristics and classifications of sticks. This will help you talk about what type of stick you've found or are rating.

ANIMAL *n* [class]: A stick that resembles an animal.

ARTIFACT *n* [class]: A stick that does not have a utility function, but is used as adornment or decoration, often mystic in origin.

ARTILLERY *n* [class]: A stick that resembles ranged weaponry (that is, weapons that require ammunition), such as a bow and arrow, pistol, cannon, or laser gun, or a wielded weapon such as a boomerang or slingshot.

BLUDGEON *n* [class]: A stick that resembles a type of clubbing object, such as a hammer, mace, or cudgel.

CANE *n* [class]: A stick that serves as a functional walking aid. Ideally, a cane stick is long enough to reach from the ground to the user's hip and has an ergonomic handle at the head of the stick. Notable cane stick: Willy Wonka's cane.

DEFENSE *n* [class]: Typically broad and wide, a stick that serves as a protection, such as a shield or armor.

MODDED *adj* [class]: A stick that has been modified or altered from its natural state. These alterations can affect various attributes of the stick, including its texture, durability, and overall functionality.

NATTY *adj* [class]: A stick that remains in its natural state, without any modifications, treatments, or alterations.

NUDE *adj* [class]: A stick that has been stripped of its bark, leaving the underlying wood exposed.

POLEARM *n* [class]: A stick that resembles any type of bladed shaft object such as a spear, scythe, or pickaxe.

STAFF *n* [class]: A stick that resembles a staff in terms of form and function, characterized by its length, diameter, and sturdiness. Typically used for trekking on journeys and occasionally casting magic. Notable staff stick: Gandalf's staff from *The Lord of the Rings*.

STASH *n* [class]: A group of sticks.

SWORD *n* [class]: A stick that resembles various types of bladed objects.

WAND *n* [class]: A slender stick, typically less than 12 inches, with a slightly tapered diameter, used primarily for magical or ceremonial purposes. Occasionally modded with ornamental features such as carvings, inscriptions, or gemstones. Notable wand sticks: the Elder Wand from the *Harry Potter* series.

WONKY *n* [class]: A stick that features asymmetrical shapes, unexpected bends, or unusual textures that contribute to its distinctive and whimsical appearance. A wonky stick possesses a charming and playful nature.

STICK TRAITS AND ATTRIBUTES

So you've classified your stick. But there are so many other elements of a stick—traits and attributes that contribute to its overall caliber, functionality, and desirability. Learning about these will help you observe, analyze, and talk about what you love (or don't love!) about your stick.

AURA: The distinctive allure and magical quality possessed by a stick, characterized by its unique presence and charm. This is the most important attribute we look for in a stick.

BALANCE: How evenly weight is distributed along the length of a stick.

BEND: The ability of a stick to flex with force while still retaining its original form.

BLUDGEONING CAPABILITIES: The stick's natural ability to deliver impact or forceful strikes.

CURVE: The degree to which a stick deviates from a straight line; its curvature.

DURABILITY: The ability of a stick to withstand stress, environmental factors, and wear over time.

GRAIN: The alignment, arrangement, and pattern of the fibers within a stick.

GRIP: How comfortably and securely a user can hold and control a stick.

LENGTH: The measurement of a stick from end to end.

MYSTICAL CAPABILITIES: The natural attributes of a stick that go beyond the physical and enter the realm of the magical and supernatural.

PIERCING CAPABILITIES: The stick's natural ability to penetrate or puncture another material.

QUIRK: The unique, wonky, charming, or distinctive traits of a stick.

SLASHING CAPABILITIES: The stick's natural ability to cut or slice through materials when swung.

SNAP: The sound and vibration created when a stick fractures.

SPIN: The rotation of a stick around its own axis.

WEIGHT: The mass of the stick. This can be measured in pounds, kilograms, or ounces, but the most important determination of weight is how the stick feels in your hand.

GALLERY OF STICKS

The heart of this book is the simplicity of people and their connection with sticks. So we decided to let the members of Stick Nation speak for themselves.

We asked the Stick Nation community to send in photos of their favorite sticks, along with any anecdotes they would like to share. They did not disappoint. In just three months, we received thousands of stick submissions from all over the world. From the shores of Scotland, to the Himalayan mountains, to the outback of Australia, to the rainforests of Chile—people sent in stick photos from every corner of the globe.

The following is a collection of photos and anecdotes from real members of Stick Nation.

We are honored to showcase this global community and collection of sticks. We hope you feel the joy of nature and the simple magic of being human as you explore these sticks. Feel free to rate each on your own!

FOUND BY **KATHARINA** · LOCATION **PACIFIC NORTHWEST COAST, UNITED STATES** · CLASS **STAFF**

This one lives by my front door; it's my Welcoming Staff. I believe it wards off bad vibes and keeps my house safe!

I feel like this stick-bench was made with the sole purpose to be in the Stick Nation book.

FOUND BY **ANIKA-GRACE AND SOPHIE**
LOCATION **LANCASHIRE, UK**
CLASS **WONKY STAFF**

It's a cool stick we found on an adventure in the woods. It could be a bow, it could be a staff, or it could be lightning!

FOUND BY **EVA**
LOCATION **VALLORBE, SWITZERLAND**
CLASS **STAFF**

We were camping by the Lac de Joux and drove to Vallorbe to see these huge caves. My son found this stick right by the caves, next to the River Orbe. The stick was very heavy and wet, but he was so happy having it and carried it back to our car, and now he plays with it in front of our caravan.

FOUND BY **SIWOH**
LOCATION **THE NETHERLANDS**
CLASS **NATTY**

My kids love sticks.

FOUND BY **ELLIOT**
LOCATION **PASO ROBLES,
CALIFORNIA, UNITED STATES**
CLASS **NATTY**

My name is Elliot. I am 1, and I recently got into stick finding. While at the farmers market I found this epic stick that was the perfect weight/length ratio to my body and I carried it around for 3 days before the ocean ultimately reclaimed it.

FOUND BY **NASSIM**
LOCATION **LAC DE BUCLET, FRANCE**
CLASS **NATTY**

This is my daughter's first big stick, a very nice one!

FOUND BY **KUNTHI**
LOCATION **SANUR, BALI, INDONESIA**
CLASS **STAFF**

According to my daughter, this stick is a hat rack. A powerful hat rack! We found it on the beach, and it has a fossil-like color. Quite heavy, perfect for defense! (We don't wanna attack anyone . . .)

FOUND BY **BRIANA**
LOCATION **ARKANSAS, UNITED STATES**
CLASS **NATTY**

Found this stick while at Grandma's river cabin. It met an honorable end keeping us warm that night.

FOUND BY **KHALID**
LOCATION **CAMEROON**
CLASS **NATTY**

My son went out with his mom and
brought home a stick, safe and sound.

FOUND BY **MUUL**
LOCATION **COSTA RICA**
CLASS **WONKY**

On a chill day with my friend on a yacht
in Costa Rica, I swam to the beach,
and after a while of looking around I
found a peculiar stick. I called it
"stick of wisdom." The shape of its
surroundings—it's perfect—brought
me joy and excitement for the future
adventure with it.

FOUND BY **ASH**
LOCATION **SOUTHERN CALIFORNIA,
UNITED STATES**
CLASS **STAFF**

This stick is very tall, standing at 6 feet 3 inches, and smooth all around. Very nice hiking stick. I love sticks. #sticknation4life

FOUND BY **SERGIO**
LOCATION **ITALY**
CLASS **STAFF**

This is my father, Sergio, and this is his stick. He is from Blera, Italy. He found the stick in the woods. He needed to have dinner with other people, so he hid his stick very well so it could not be stolen. On his way home, my father kept stopping random people to say the stick was solid and very heavy, useful for walking, and will end up in the stove this winter. He was so happy with his stick.

FOUND BY **GIORGIO**
LOCATION **SAN NAZZARO, SWITZERLAND**
CLASS **NATTY**

A beautiful stick found on the shores of Lago Maggiore. Beautiful yet with a tragic history, as it has appeared after a devastating storm which caused some casualties and enormous damage. It's a reminder of Mother Nature's dichotomy between beautifulness and dangerousness.

FOUND BY **CHARLES**
LOCATION **OHIO, UNITED STATES**
CLASS **NATTY**

I Love Sticks.

FOUND BY **YOGESH**
LOCATION **SEDONA,
ARIZONA, UNITED STATES**
CLASS **NATTY**

Found this stick on a trail.

FOUND BY **CHRISTELE**
LOCATION **INDIANA,**
UNITED STATES
CLASS **STAFF**

I'm usually a no-frills-stick type of hiker, but this stick had too much character to pass by! With its two-pronged head, some intricate knobby bits, and a whole lot of personality, I feel like this stick's got stories to tell—and scars to prove it! It looks like it's been in the thick of battle, fought off fierce foes, and survived to tell the tale. But now, it's ready to hang up its armor and take on quieter adventures. No more charging into the fray, no more clashing steel—just peaceful strolls, gentle streams, and maybe a picnic or two. It's like it's saying, "I've earned my rest, but I'm not done exploring just yet!"

FOUND BY **BALAZS AND DANIEL**
LOCATION **HUNGARY**
CLASS **CANE**

Love Stick Nation. Like we all used to as children, now even though we grew up, their magic remained the same. Nice to see that I'm not alone with it!

FOUND BY **FREDDIE**
LOCATION **CARMARTHEN, WALES**
CLASS **STAFF**

I found this stick while walking the 870-mile Wales Coast Path last year. It saw me through mud and rain and many many miles, and I have regretted rashly abandoning it ever since.

FOUND BY **DHEN**
LOCATION **MOUNT WILIS,
EAST JAVA, INDONESIA**
CLASS **CANE**

I felt my aura increase
and it helped my climbing
skills and I was able to
conquer Jontani Peak at
an altitude of 1,596 meters
above sea level.

FOUND BY **NAREG**
LOCATION **YOSEMITE NATIONAL PARK,
CALIFORNIA, UNITED STATES**
CLASS **STAFF**

I found this stick on a 20-mile hike to El Capitan in Yosemite. After about 4 miles of hiking, my legs were getting weak and my spirit was growing weary. I was strongly considering abandoning the objective and turning back. Lo and behold, this mystical staff appeared to me in my time of need. Garnished with intricate markings from bark beetles (or ancient alien civilizations, who knows?), this staff gave me the extra support needed to carry on, navigate the difficult terrain, and reach my destination safely. It's very sturdy, and the surface markings offer great grip while hiking. It has loads of character and will accompany me on many future hikes to come.

FOUND BY **LUKE**
LOCATION **ATHERTON, AUSTRALIA**
CLASS **MODDED**

About 10 years ago, I was living in Australia and I had a Chilean couple stay with me (couch surfing). They gifted me "The Stick" and said that I was the Stick Master now. The rules of Stick Master were simple:

1. Take the stick on your travels.
2. Take photos of the stick in various Loot Locations and post to the stick group.
3. When you are no longer traveling, carve your mark onto the stick and pass the stick on to a new master.

The group is now dormant, and the last known Loot Location of the stick is hanging behind a bar in a pub in Australia. Overall, it had 8 masters and traveled 20,000 km.

FOUND BY **JIJO**
LOCATION **PALAKKAD, KERALA, INDIA**
CLASS **ARTIFACT AND DEFENSE**

The fantasy sticks.

FOUND BY **MANU**
LOCATION **SIRSI, KARNATAKA, INDIA**
CLASS **MODDED SWORD**

A katana-shaped stick, used for slashing and thrashing of wild plants. Additional custom grip is provided by its enemies' skin.

FOUND BY **VADIM**
LOCATION **LAKE BAIKAL, IRKUTSK, RUSSIA**
CLASS **NATTY**

This stick was found quite by accident. We were vacationing on the shore of the Bratsk reservoir and decided with a friend to take an inflatable boat to the other shore, where this stick was found. It played a huge role in our trip; with its help a large number of local jokes were born. We brought it back to the city and beautifully fit this find into the interior of the apartment. It became one of the main symbols of our two-week trip and now we will always remember it. On the stick itself, you can see incredibly beautiful patterns that resemble the streams of rivers.

FOUND BY **TEA**
LOCATION **FINLAND**
CLASS **STASH**

Every stick was picked from a different Loot Location on my road trip. Some are from forest, some beach, and some from a riverside. Various shapes, sizes, and uses.

FOUND BY **EMMY**
LOCATION **NORWAY**
CLASS **STASH**

It's been curated in a black plastic bag for more than 10 years. Took it out and it balances perfectly in my hands. It's a magic stick! Ended up emptying my "crow's nest," and this is the result.

FOUND BY **AMANDA**
LOCATION **COALBROOKDALE, UK**
CLASS **STASH**

It's a shop for every kind of stick.
It's stick heaven.

FOUND BY **JOSHUA**
LOCATION **COLUMBUS, OHIO,
UNITED STATES**
CLASS **STASH**

This is not one stick, but MULTIPLE
sticks that some kind people have
left for others to use at the trailhead
in one of our metro parks!

FOUND BY **CARLOS**
LOCATION **CHAMPAIGN,
ILLINOIS, UNITED STATES**
CLASS **STASH**

Stick station!

FOUND BY **TRAVIS**
LOCATION **VICTORIA,
BRITISH COLUMBIA,
CANADA**
CLASS **BLUDGEON**

This stick looks like a magical
hammer from mythology.
Found on the beach on the
west coast of Graham Island.

FOUND BY **ELI**
LOCATION **COORDINATES:
37.8037°, -122.4574°**
CLASS **STASH**

This is a stick fort made
using multiple different
sticks which we found in
a park. This stick fort was
well made, with a roof and
small sticks as a path for
decoration. We also found
a large stick, which can be
used as a staff or a walking
stick, which I am holding
in the picture.

FOUND BY **ANTONELLA**
LOCATION **CORTINA D'AMPEZZO, ITALY**
CLASS **FORT**

A beautiful
House of Sticks
in the Dolomites.

FOUND BY **ROBYN**
LOCATION **PRINCE EDWARD ISLAND, CANADA**
CLASS **STASH**

This is actually 3 awesome sticks that my eleven-year-old son gathered, then balanced on the beach. On their own, each stick had great feel and balance, but together, they highlight the elegance of a good stick!

FOUND BY **MINGO**
LOCATION **KIAWAH ISLAND,
SOUTH CAROLINA, UNITED STATES**
CLASS **STASH**

This is my pile of sticks I collected on my walks! I like to visit it periodically to make sure it's still amazing (it always is).

FOUND BY **MURPH**
LOCATION **TALLAHASSEE,
FLORIDA, UNITED STATES**
CLASS **NATTY**

It's not really about the one stick;
it's about the stick lifestyle.

FOUND BY **KRISTI**
LOCATION **POWERS PARK, PORT
RICHMOND, PHILADELPHIA,
PENNSYLVANIA, UNITED STATES**
CLASS **NATTY**

My dog Frankie always likes to
find the biggest sticks on his
walks around our neighborhood.
He chewed on this particular
stick so hard he lost a tooth!

FOUND BY **LEITNER**
LOCATION **GIRONDE, FRANCE**
CLASS **STAFF**

A very old mossy wizard's staff that my three followers desire more than all others.

FOUND BY **CHARLIE**
LOCATION **BARNSLEY, SOUTH YORKSHIRE, ENGLAND**
CLASS **NATTY**

Firstly, it's a bouncy stick. When you throw it and it lands, it bounces like a ball, and it's incredibly fun to catch. We collect a stick every morning, but the bouncy stick is the main stick.

Y-shaped stick found by Buddy! Good for long-range attack with a slingshot attachment and has plus 5 magic.

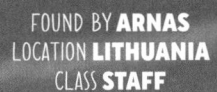

FOUND BY **ARNAS**
LOCATION **LITHUANIA**
CLASS **STAFF**

It's clean, it's simple, and it's robust—it's a true druid's stick! The model comes dust- and dirt-free, 100% organic, and BPA free!

FOUND BY **EDUARDO**
LOCATION **GARUVA, SANTA CATARINA, BRAZIL**
CLASS **NUDE NATTY**

I found this amazing stick hiking on a beautiful Sunday morning.

FOUND BY **JAYA**
LOCATION **MIDDLE OF NOWHERE**
CLASS **ARTILLERY**

This was found on the top of a mountain.

FOUND BY **ARCHER**
LOCATION **EDGEWOOD,
WASHINGTON,
UNITED STATES**
CLASS **NATTY**

The Wishbone Stick. We have used to prop open numerous things. A very versatile stick.

FOUND BY **DAN'S DAUGHTER**
LOCATION **TOFINO, BRITISH
COLUMBIA, CANADA**
CLASS **NATTY**

My daughter found the emperor stick. Only the most powerful can wield such a mighty stick. Multipurpose of course. Sticks will save the world!

FOUND BY **MALIK** • LOCATION **ACEH, INDONESIA** • CLASS **POLEARM**

Hello Stick Nation, my name is Malik, I'm 10 years old from Indonesia. I found this cool stick when I was trekking to the jungle in Banda Aceh, Indonesia. I think you can catch a rat using the Y-shaped edge. And if you are trekking to the mountain or to the jungle you can take a break by resting your head in the Y-shaped edge. Thanks Stick Nation.

FOUND BY **CONSTABLE MARCHAND**
LOCATION **LONDON, ONTARIO, CANADA**
CLASS **ARTILLERY**

As crime rates soar, police services are looking for creative new ways to stick it to criminals who disobey the law. The streets are unforgiving, so I make sure never to leave my cruiser without my long, pronged stick of the law, towering at over nine feet high. One look at this monstrosity of justice sends would-be criminals running for the hills. This stick's innovative Y shape enables me to fend off multiple bad guys at once, and can easily be fashioned into a slingshot capable of firing rounds no pistol could match. Soon all police services will have branches dedicated to developing the latest in stick-based crime-fighting devices. For now, I know I am safe as long as I have ol' reliable in my hands.

FOUND BY **KATHARINE AND MATTHEW**
LOCATION **THETFORD FOREST, NORFOLK, UK**
CLASS **NATTY**

On a foggy New Year's walk, my brother Matthew went missing. We were very lucky to see him return within two minutes, but not alone— with a tremendously impressive stick twice his size. We discussed what should be done with such a large specimen.

FOUND BY **RYAN**
LOCATION **MALVERN HILLS, ENGLAND**
CLASS **NATTY**

One breezy afternoon on the Malvern Hills, our football rolled hundreds of meters away. Determined, we sprinted after it, hearts pounding, feet barely touching the ground. Just when hope seemed lost, the McBall led us to a majestic stick, standing three times my height, resting against a tree as if waiting for us.

FOUND BY **JACOPO**
LOCATION **GREECE**
CLASS **NATTY**

Beautiful stick. Tall and heavy.
A particular shape which seems
to rotate on itself, and impressive
dimension, more than 4 meters.

FOUND BY **KALEB**
LOCATION **NORTH CAROLINA,
UNITED STATES**
CLASS **NATTY**

Me and my boys were taking a
stroll in the woods and the stick
was on the ground, so I just picked
it up and told my boy to take a
picture of me because I thought
it was majestical.

FOUND BY **HUGO AND TILLY**
LOCATION **SYDNEY, AUSTRALIA**
CLASS **WONKY**

We found this stick near the park we
go to. It has a small hold at the end,
smooth exterior, super straight and
super big. If you lean it up against
a rock, it makes a great footrest or a
place to sit. Put it over a fallen tree
log and you've got yourself a seesaw!

FOUND BY **DANIEL**
LOCATION **ŠPINDLERŮV MLÝN, CZECH REPUBLIC**
CLASS **STAFF**

I believe this is a magical staff, just missing a crystal on top! Maybe it belonged to an ancient wizard. Now it can serve as a catcher, until the right crystal is found.

FOUND BY **JON**
LOCATION **PAXSON, ALASKA, UNITED STATES**
CLASS **POLEARM**

Found it on the bed of a river; couldn't fly back with it, so I gave it to a kid.

FOUND BY **GRANT**
LOCATION **BEACH NEAR KILLARA, AUSTRALIA**
CLASS **NATTY**

It was very tall but still sticky. My child is also holding a stick.

FOUND BY **SAVANNA**
LOCATION **KAUAI, HAWAII**
CLASS **NATTY**

My stick is a beautiful bamboo specimen.
Very tall, very smooth!

FOUND BY **CODY**
LOCATION **BRITISH COLUMBIA, CANADA**
CLASS **STAFF**

It was 9:30 p.m. Heat wave.
Fortuitously found a perfect staff
floating. Had to snap a photo.

FOUND BY **CLEMENT** • LOCATION **KENT DOWNS AREA OF OUTSTANDING NATURAL BEAUTY (AONB) NEAR WYE, KENT, UK** • CLASS **ARTIFACT**

It's an incredible stick with a gentle bend and a spiral effect midway up its length. Another plant had wrapped around the stick, constricting it in such a way that the spiral pattern was formed.

FOUND BY **AARON**
LOCATION **THE BAHAMAS**
CLASS **WONKY**

It's long and wavy.

FOUND BY **OTIS**
LOCATION **MARBELLA, SPAIN**
CLASS **STAFF**

It's a big stick. It's probably an 8-foot stick. I'm only 4 feet.

FOUND BY **HOLLY**
LOCATION **DEVON, ENGLAND**
CLASS **WONKY STAFF**

My stick is an 8-foot-tall staff! Clearly very powerful. Its wonky end is perfect for impaling things. Finding cool sticks makes me feel better when I've had a rough day.

FOUND BY **PAWEL**
LOCATION **NIESZAWA, POLAND**
CLASS **NATTY**

Beech tree stick; found it in a
five-years-old pile of wood/
sticks. Extremely solid, universal,
multipurpose stick.

FOUND BY **KAREN**
LOCATION **MAROON BELLS,
COLORADO, UNITED STATES**
CLASS **STAFF**

I found my stick while sitting on
the banks of the Roaring Fork River
in May of 2021. I spied it caught
in a shallow eddy, so I walked out
into the cold water and grabbed
it. It is weighted perfectly, with a
natural handhold and foot grip.
Fellow travelers comment on the
greatness of the Stick. They say,
"That is a great stick." I have never
named the Stick, for I think it
surpasses any I could think of.

FOUND BY **MIMI**
LOCATION **MICHIGAN
CITY, INDIANA,
UNITED STATES**
CLASS **NATTY**

Big beach stick.
Found vertical.

FOUND BY **ANSHUL**
LOCATION **INDIA**
CLASS **SACRED RELIC**

In the ancient Himalayan foothills, a young shepherd named Arun discovered a mystical bamboo stick known as Vayusparsha, blessed by Vayu, the god of the wind. During a violent storm, Arun, trapped with his flock on a narrow ledge, grasped the stick and miraculously calmed the winds, guiding them to safety. Recognized for its divine power to control the weather and communicate with air spirits, Vayusparsha became a sacred relic, enshrined in its grove and revered by pilgrims seeking protection and blessings. The stick in the image could be a piece of this legendary bamboo, holding within it the breath of the wind god.

FOUND BY **ALEJANDRO GARCIA SANCHO GARAYZAR**
LOCATION **ENSENADA, BAJA CALIFORNIA, MEXICO**
CLASS **STAFF**

Hiking the Cañón de Doña Petra Trail, we found an amazing stick with flowers attached to the top part. I see a lot of resemblance with the biblical Aaron's Rod, in which, by the grace of God, flowers blossomed in the staff, symbolizing a lot of things, but the most popular states that God chose Aaron and his tribe to carry His Holy Work. Great level of mysticism and magic.

FOUND BY **SAM**
LOCATION **BRISBANE,
AUSTRALIA**
CLASS **WAND**

As I was walking home from school,
I found a stick that looks identical
to that of a wand in *Harry Potter*.

FOUND BY **CHAZ**
LOCATION **LEEDS,
WEST YORKSHIRE, ENGLAND**
CLASS **STAFF**

A wizard staff found deep in the
countryside. Sticks hold a deeper
meaning. If you find such a stick,
it was but meant to be.

FOUND BY **VUKASIN**
LOCATION **SERBIA**
CLASS **WAND**

The thousand-pierced stick found in the backyard.

FOUND BY **AARON**
LOCATION **COMUNITÀ DELLA
VALLAGARINA, ITALY**
CLASS **NATTY**

I happened upon this stick on a
whimsical journey. It bonded with
my hand and we became one. As
you can see, it is truly one of a kind.

FOUND BY **SUSAN**
LOCATION **DENVER, COLORADO,
UNITED STATES**
CLASS **NATTY**

A photo of me holding a mossy
stick with my arm outstretched. On
my arm is a tattoo of a stick being
held by an arm outstretched.

FOUND BY **POLITI**
LOCATION **FRANCE**
CLASS **MODDED**

This boxwood stick was given to me by a friend; it offered me a really interesting, solid, and durable base. Before working on this stick, it took me time, and then one day I wanted to sculpt without really knowing how or what to do. That's when I started working one day in channeling, and the more I advanced, the more this face appeared.

FOUND BY **OLIVER**
LOCATION **NEW FOREST, ENGLAND**
CLASS **MODDED WAND**

It was a very old twisty stick shaped perfectly like a wand, so I attached a green crystal to the end and made it look like a real wizard's wand. The end has a really interesting spiral, and the body has a nicely shaped handle.

FOUND BY **MARTINS**
LOCATION **JURMALCIEMS BEACH, LATVIA**
CLASS **NATTY**

With my daughter, I found this stick washed up on the seashore. We brought it home, and it has been with us for a year, moving from room to room. It's become a part of our family. That stick simply enjoys our company. We love it!

FOUND BY **ELIJAH**
LOCATION **SACO, MAINE, UNITED STATES**
CLASS **WONKY**

I like sticks. They are cool.
My mom doesn't like when
I bring them in the house.

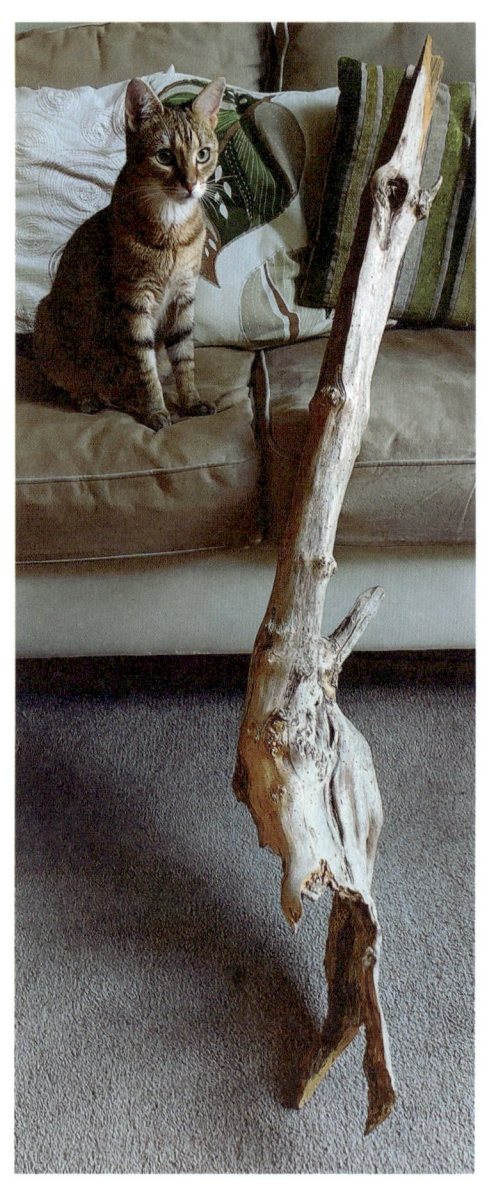

FOUND BY **FIONA**
LOCATION **WALES, UK**
CLASS **NATTY**

I found it at the Glade Festival in Houghton Hall, Norfolk, England. It was a random stick in the field where we were camping. It's weathered like it had been in the elements for a while . . . and possibly from cows chewing it.

FOUND BY **NICK**
LOCATION **HILVERSUM,
THE NETHERLANDS**
CLASS **WONKY**

I found this stick and it immediately
looked like leather, but with the
feeling of a fine and strong stick.
I love this piece.

FOUND BY **KALLE**
LOCATION **KURU, FINLAND**
CLASS **STAFF AND BLUDGEON**

It's a 100-year-old Finnish walking stick/bludgeon made by my great grandfather. It's used as a walking stick and a weapon if necessary. It's called *ryhmysauva* in Finnish.

FOUND BY **RAIDHER**
LOCATION **DOMINICAN REPUBLIC**
CLASS **NATTY**

In 2020, while riding my motorcycle, I heard a thunderous
sound that made me stop. I looked toward the small forest
where the noise came from. I saw that this beautiful stick had
fallen from a century-old tree. Without hesitation, I took it and
carried it with me on my motorcycle. It has been with me for
four years now, residing in my central office where I work.

FOUND BY **SOHAIB**
LOCATION **MOROCCO**
CLASS **WONKY**

While looking for driftwood
for my aquarium, I found this
stick that has amazing
it. Currently in an
ome.

FOUND BY **JOHN**
LOCATION **HARBOR COVE
BEACH, VENTURA,
CALIFORNIA,
UNITED STATES**
CLASS **ANIMAL**

Looks a lot like a seahorse.

FOUND BY **MELISSA**
LOCATION **ASHEVILLE,
NORTH CAROLINA,
UNITED STATES**
CLASS **ANIMAL**

Found my cute little stick
buddy while walking in
the woods having a sad
day. Cheered me up right
away. I needed a friend.

FOUND BY **BENJAMIN**
LOCATION **LIMASSOL,
CYPRUS**
CLASS **ANIMAL**

I found this amazing
crocodile-shaped stick on
a beach in Cyprus.

FOUND BY **SIMÃO**
LOCATION **ALGARVE,
PORTUGAL**
CLASS **ANIMAL**

It is perfectly shaped like
a velociraptor claw.

FOUND BY **INDIVÍDUO**
LOCATION **VOUZELA, PORTUGAL**
CLASS **ANIMAL**

It looks like an animal, but it's a stick. I bring it
home, give it a bath, a little skin care, and that's it.

FOUND BY **RYAN**
LOCATION **KENORA, ONTARIO, CANADA**
CLASS **ANIMAL**

Long-tailed rat/weasel stick with 4 legs

FOUND BY **SIMÃO**
LOCATION **ALGARVE,
PORTUGAL**
CLASS **ANIMAL**

Chicken paw!!

When my son was little, my mom and I took him on a walk and found
this stick. My mom said it looked like a monkey claw, and we took it
home. My son is now 40, and I still have the monkey claw—however,
I just passed it on to him this year. He keeps it on a shelf.

FOUND BY **ALEKA**
LOCATION **BALI, INDONESIA**
CLASS **STAFF**

Two-headed snake staff.

FOUND BY **KEVIN**
LOCATION **INDIA**
CLASS **STAFF**

Ophidian Scepter: It's a staff used by the leader of ancient tribes who used to worship the snake lord. It resembles the head of a snake.

FOUND BY **AMANDA**
LOCATION **LAKE MICHIGAN AND SISKIYOU COUNTY, CALIFORNIA, UNITED STATES**
CLASS **MODDED**

For the last 12 years I have been finding sticks on hikes that look like snakes and painting them to resemble real snake species. A friend had gotten a "root snake," which is a Southern folk art tradition, and I became obsessed and wanted to make my own. Sticks in the photos include Blue Ribbon Snake, California Mountain Kingsnake, Albino Milk Snake, San Francisco Garter Snake, and Banded Krait.

FOUND BY **MEHEK**
LOCATION **LONDON**
CLASS **ARTIFACT**

Fallen stick/s on the ground after a breeze. Found a paper clip earlier in the day also on the road and made what I called a seating arrangement for fairies using flat sticks, curved sticks, branch outer layer coverings (used as a shade that is balanced on the stick), bird feather, and discarded paper clip and bottle opener. *Why have one stick when you can have many?* led me to making something super silly. It sits on my bedside table now.

FOUND BY **SILVIA**
LOCATION **ITALY**
CLASS **MODDED WAND**

My stick is a forked wand, cut from a medlar tree located in my garden, that has been debarked and decorated with sea-themed charms. There is a starfish pendant, a light-blue feather, little seashells and pearl buttons hanging from the back, and a sun charm that was gifted to me when I was very little. It has a beautiful white finish, and it is a powerful tool to summon sirens from the sea! Blessed by Neptune and friend to all MerPeople!

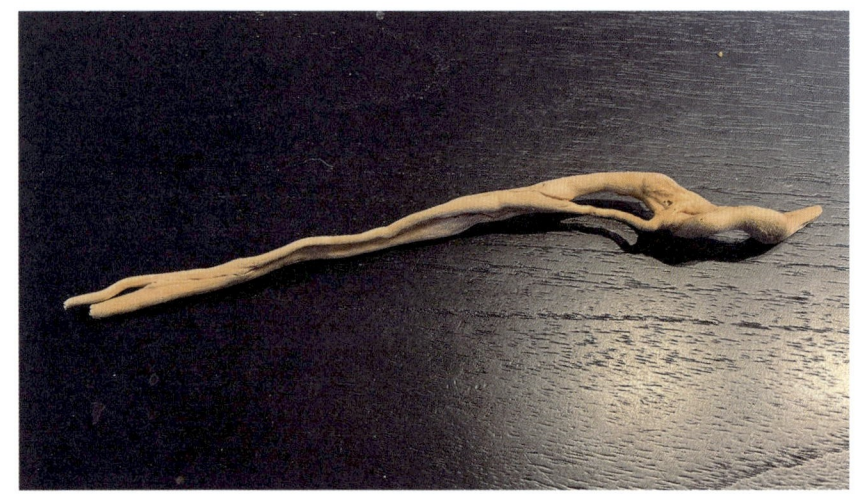

FOUND BY **MICHELLE**
LOCATION **BURLINGTON, ONTARIO, CANADA**
CLASS **FINGER**

This stick obviously was once the finger of an Ent. I'm not sure how he lost it, but he was nowhere to be found. I will hold it for him in case he comes for it.

I found it in the Cévennes, in France, and then I used a Swiss Army knife to make it look like a thumb.

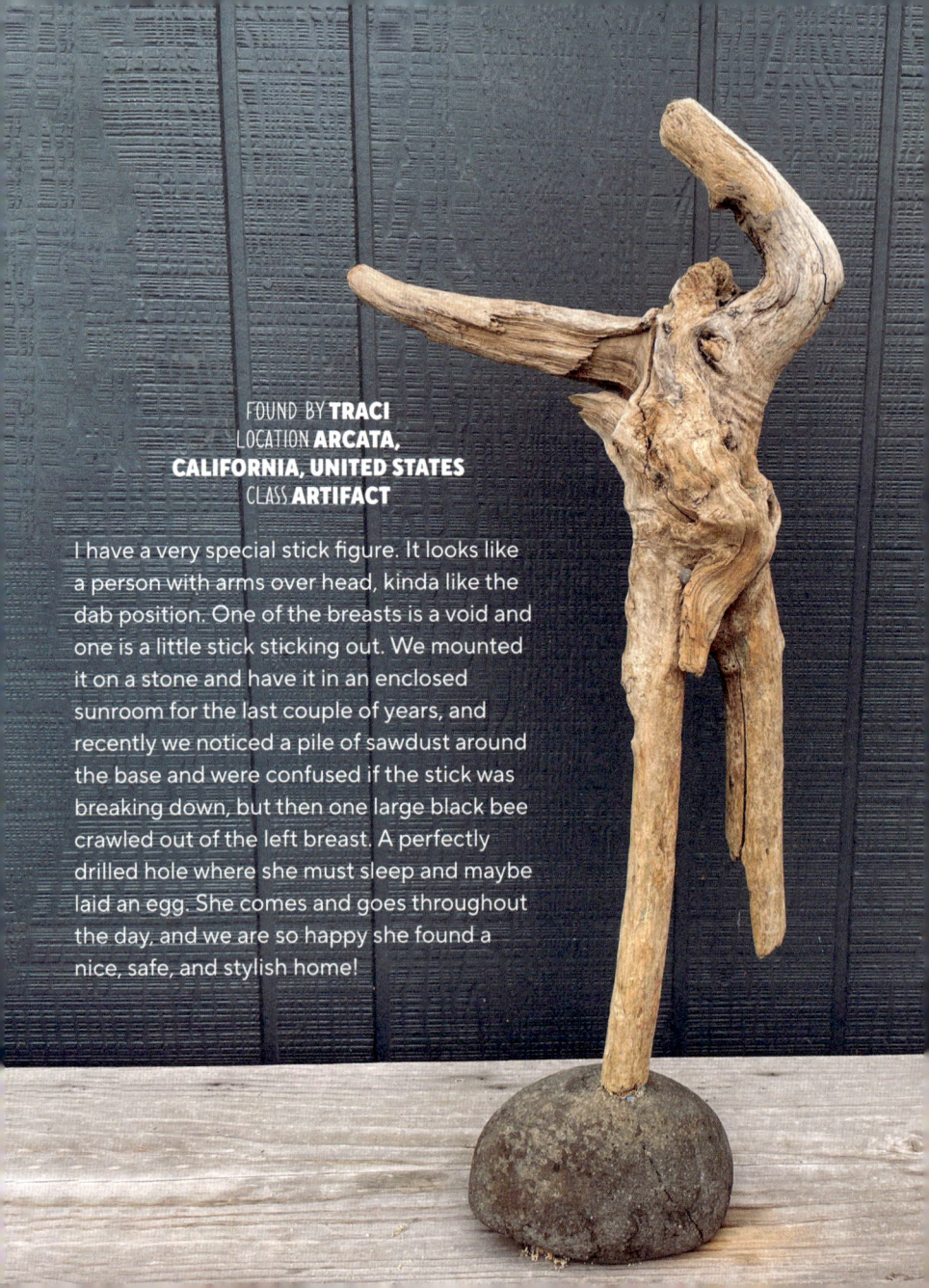

FOUND BY **TRACI**
LOCATION **ARCATA,
CALIFORNIA, UNITED STATES**
CLASS **ARTIFACT**

I have a very special stick figure. It looks like a person with arms over head, kinda like the dab position. One of the breasts is a void and one is a little stick sticking out. We mounted it on a stone and have it in an enclosed sunroom for the last couple of years, and recently we noticed a pile of sawdust around the base and were confused if the stick was breaking down, but then one large black bee crawled out of the left breast. A perfectly drilled hole where she must sleep and maybe laid an egg. She comes and goes throughout the day, and we are so happy she found a nice, safe, and stylish home!

I found this stick three years ago on the sidewalk, needing help. I picked him up and I brought him home. I called him Jacklino and took care of him. One year later he broke his arm, and I fixed it using a piece of another stick.

FOUND BY **KING LAM**
LOCATION **OLYMPIC NATIONAL PARK,
WASHINGTON, UNITED STATES**
CLASS **NATTY**

The old man and the sea! He was an old man who stood there for a long time, waiting for his son to come back from a fishing trip, and became a tree!!

FOUND BY **ROB**
LOCATION **TŌTARANUI,
NEW ZEALAND**
CLASS **NATTY**

Two sticks in love.

FOUND BY **SAANA**
LOCATION **INARI, FINLAND**
CLASS **ANIMAL**

Found it in Sápmi, the land
of the Sámi Indigenous
people. It looks like a water
snake/lil monster.

FOUND BY **MAJA**
LOCATION **FALSTER, DENMARK**
CLASS **ANIMAL**

I found this little stick in the sand by the water. I didn't see it at first, but when I came home I saw that it looks like a dragon.

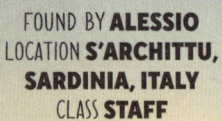

FOUND BY **ALESSIO**
LOCATION **S'ARCHITTU,**
SARDINIA, ITALY
CLASS **STAFF**

It's a magic stick that can handle
the power of the sun!

FOUND BY **PETER**
LOCATION **MOSCOW, RUSSIA**
CLASS **MODDED**

It's a magical stick, made from many other forest trees! It has the form of a hand that holds a disco ball. It can light your way and send a green light stream 2 km above to the sky!

FOUND BY **SAUMYA**
LOCATION **SULTANPUR, UTTAR PRADESH, INDIA**
CLASS **ANIMAL**

It is a sun eater. A little monster that eats the evening sun and brings on the night.

FOUND BY **GONER**
LOCATION **OGDEN, UTAH,
UNITED STATES**
CLASS **POLEARM**

This stick is a tall stick but not as tall as some other sticks. Although its range is mighty, it can only wipe out about 36 villagers in a single blow. 37? No. 38? Can't do. 39? Not a chance. 36 is the number of villagers, and 36 shall the number be. Many a villager has fallen beneath its glorious power, bones have been shattered, families torn apart, corporations completely dismantled.

FOUND BY **JOSHUA**
LOCATION **YARRA RIVER,
VICTORIA, AUSTRALIA**
CLASS **STAFF AND BLUDGEON**

Forged in the waters of the
mighty Yarra. Protruding
upright from the river
bank, ready to be pulled
from the earth as if it were
a sword in a stone. Wizard
staff abilities whilst still
retaining melee ability
with its clubbed head and
sharp end.

FOUND BY **LOGAN**
LOCATION **WEST BEND,
WISCONSIN,
UNITED STATES**
CLASS **MODDED WAND**

Found a branch with an
awesome burl on it and
wanted to make it into a
wand. It ended up looking
more like a bone, which
I think would make a great
wand for a witch.

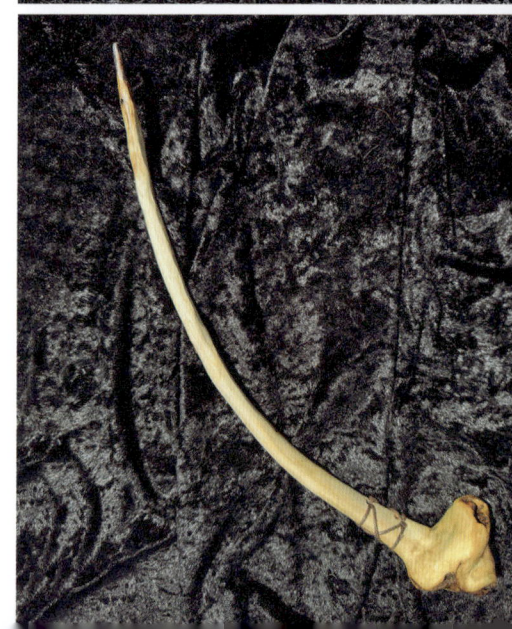

FOUND BY **BEN**
LOCATION **KINGFISHER TRAIL, WEST VIRGINIA, UNITED STATES**
CLASS **STAFF**

Sick-ass wizard staff.

FOUND BY **CALSON**
LOCATION **MALAYSIA**
CLASS **WAND**

The Long Magician Stick
with Assassin Ability.

FOUND BY **AIDEN**
LOCATION **WASATCH MOUNTAINS,
UTAH, UNITED STATES**
CLASS **STAFF**

It's an awesome
wizard lighting staff.

FOUND BY **LONNIE**
LOCATION **MORRO BAY,
CALIFORNIA, UNITED STATES**
CLASS **STAFF**

Large Dark Magic Wizard Staff
found on the beach at Morro Bay.
A ton of dark energy can be felt
while wielding this. It must have
been left by a powerful mage.

FOUND BY **MATTIA**
LOCATION **EMILIA-ROMAGNA, ITALY**
CLASS **POLEARM**

I found it while I was wandering in a small forest with my friends. It was already a cloudy day, and as soon as I took the stick with me it started to rain. A trident that summons rain? Bringing it home was a must.

FOUND BY **ADRIAN**
LOCATION **ST. CATHARINES,
ONTARIO, CANADA**
CLASS **STAFF**

It is my wizard staff that I found in a pile of driftwood on the shore of Lake Erie a few years ago. I added a wooden ring to it recently.

FOUND BY **LUCAS**
LOCATION **JURA, FRANCE**
CLASS **STAFF**

A magician stick which can also be used as a weapon.

FOUND BY **GARY**
LOCATION **UTAH, USA**
CLASS **ARTIFACT**

A stick ends up in the shape of a heart. Is it an inspiring miracle of nature or a disappointing piece of unusable wood? You get to decide if something is a gift or a gaffe. Always choose to see the miracles.

FOUND BY **SIERRA**
LOCATION **MOGOLLON RIM,
ARIZONA, UNITED STATES**
CLASS **ARTIFACT**

Sticklace of Power. Place
around the neck for night
vision and bonus defense while
traversing high desert terrain.

FOUND BY **DAVID**
LOCATION **TRIPLE PEAK,
BRITISH COLUMBIA,
CANADA**
CLASS **STAFF**

An arcane relic for
mountain wizards.

FOUND BY **NIKOLAY**
LOCATION **UKRAINE**
CLASS **WONKY**

I found this stick in the forest and was surprised by its unusual shape. The photo was taken about a year ago, and from that time only one photo remains. I came across your Instagram page and really liked the idea and originality.

FOUND BY **VINCENT**
LOCATION **DIJON, FRANCE**
CLASS **WONKY**

It's a rare stick!

FOUND BY **SILJE**
LOCATION **EASTERN NORWAY**
CLASS **WONKY**

I found it while walking in the deep forest to look at several stone ring burials. (Burials date somewhere between the Bronze Age and Viking Age.) Legend has it that one of the old gods forgot it by the burials and that it holds old magic. I can confirm.

FOUND BY **TEUN** • LOCATION **THE NETHERLANDS** • CLASS **ARTILLERY**

This stick has the most amazing bend, just like a half-moon. You can use it for archery, yoga, flying, and, of course, a walking stick with a little bounce.

FOUND BY **VREVEN**
LOCATION **BRETAGNE, BELGIUM**
CLASS **ARTILLERY**

J'ai trouvé ce beau bâton se baignant dans une petit crique de Bretagne. J'ai décidé de l'adopter et de le ramener visiter la Belgique.

FOUND BY **BEN**
LOCATION **MAGNOLIA, TEXAS, UNITED STATES**
CLASS **ARTILLERY**

It looks like a bow.
Sticks are everything.

FOUND BY **BLAKE**
LOCATION **BANKS PENINSULA, NEW ZEALAND**
CLASS **ARTILLERY**

A beautiful specimen shaped by the roaring seas of the Pacific, found on the beaches of the stunning Banks Peninsula, New Zealand. A fantastic curvature that sparks a budding archer in everyone who wields this mighty stick. Legolas has nothing on this beauty—its accuracy, figure, and prowess make him look like a chump.

Speed 8/10 · Flexibility 9/10
Shape 10/10

FOUND BY **HASHIR**
LOCATION **PAKISTAN**
CLASS **WONKY**

It's a cool flexible stick.
I named him "Coiled Lasso."

FOUND BY **TOM**
LOCATION **MANNINGTREE, ESSEX, UK**
CLASS **WONKY**

The stick is a piece of ivy I found while walking the dog, wrapped around a fallen tree.

FOUND BY **NATALIE**
LOCATION **BONNEVILLE SHORELINE TRAIL, UTAH, UNITED STATES**
CLASS **WONKY**

I thought this stick looked really neat.

FOUND BY **ŠARŪNAS**
LOCATION **GESALAI
GEOMORPHOLOGICAL
RESERVE, LITHUANIA**
CLASS **WONKY**

I found this stick while mushroom-
ing in Gesalai Geomorphological
Reserve. It is from a pine. It is
strangely twisted, and the surface
is quite brittle because of the
extended exposure to the elements.
To describe its shape, I would say
that it looks like a failed fusion
between a longsword and a staff.

FOUND BY **ALICE**
LOCATION **VERMONT,
UNITED STATES**
CLASS **STAFF**

This stick is so beautiful, it reminded
me of a wizard staff. It was found
by a wizard himself! He wanted me
to upload this to show off his wizard
stick to the world.

FOUND BY **WINIFRED BALBONI**
LOCATION **LAKE TEKAPO WATERFRONT, NEW ZEALAND**
CLASS **NATTY**

My father, Winifred Balboni (pictured), is a surf legend in
the small town of Lake Tekapo in Aotearoa, New Zealand.
While searching for a rumored glacial surf break on the
shoreline, he stumbled on this relic of the past. It is an ancient
matagouri bush [*Discaria toumatou*], a key feature of the
pristine landscape, and until recently it was submerged in the
azure blue depths. It now stands pride of place outside his
bungalow on the waterfront.

FOUND BY **JESPER**
LOCATION **ODDA, NORWAY**
CLASS **NATTY**

I saw it on my way home
from a swim and thought
that an opportunity like this
comes once in a lifetime.

FOUND BY **AMBRA** • LOCATION **TORRES DEL PAINE NATIONAL PARK, MAGALLANES, CHILEAN PATAGONIA** • CLASS **DEFENSE**

Dear Stick Nation, I believe this beautiful specimen was the root complex of a Ñirre or lenga beech tree in southern Chile, where all the trees are misshapen because of the constant wind. This root complex is very mesmerizing and forms a sort of lace shield to defend the user from chupacabras, wicked witches, and unwanted UFO abductions.

FOUND BY **FELIX**
LOCATION **NORWAY**
CLASS **DEFENSE**

Troll Spider—enchanted forest shield. Found in the mystical forest on the steep slopes of the Malmangernuten mountain that rises up from the fjords below.

FOUND BY **MARIA**
LOCATION **OTTAWA, CANADA**
CLASS **NATTY**

Perfect weight, the right amount
of moss, absolutely beautiful.

FOUND BY **VICTORIA**
LOCATION **KAMCHIA RIVER
ESTUARY, BULGARIA**
CLASS **BLUDGEON**

We found this cool stick on the
beach; it got washed up after a
storm. It looks very appropriate for
a weapon! It's about 1.5 meters tall,
with a spiky top and barnacles on
it. Super heavy too!

FOUND BY **CARLOS** • LOCATION **RIO GRANDE DO SUL, BRAZIL**
CLASS **WONKY**

An old bergamot tree was dying from a fungus that developed from lack of sunlight. She left this stick, her thorns sticking out like she was saying "I will fight back!" The most incredible part of all this is that there's not a bit of that fungus on this stick!

FOUND BY **MARC**
LOCATION **MORONG, RIZAL, PHILIPPINES**
CLASS **BLUDGEON**

Thorny stick.

FOUND BY **RYAN**
LOCATION **BRATTLEBORO,
VERMONT, UNITED STATES**
CLASS **NATTY**

It's a good stick! Many
pronged, very powerful!

FOUND BY **LINDA**
LOCATION **HOWARDIAN LOCAL**
NATURE RESERVE, CARDIFF, WALES
CLASS **BLUDGEON**

Clearly a very dark and powerful stick that can be used to both cast magick and just completely batter an opponent. It's very weighty and thrilling to wield. Not sure if brandishing it for a quick photo has resulted in some cataclysmic butterfly effect— there seems to be a lot of unrest in nature lately.

FOUND BY **ZOE**
LOCATION **ACADIA NATIONAL PARK,
MAINE, UNITED STATES**
CLASS **NATTY**

I found this driftwood torch while hiking the edge of the water and had to adorn it with a magic stone.

FOUND BY **HOLLAND**
LOCATION **MOAB, UTAH,
UNITED STATES**
CLASS **ARTIFACT**

Majestic stick from an
unknown mythical tree.
Probably absorbs
souls or something.

FOUND BY **BIRDIE**
LOCATION **BELLEVILLE, ILLINOIS, UNITED STATES**
CLASS **WAND AND ARTIFACT**

It reminds me of a wizard's wand or perhaps a hag stone. Good stick.

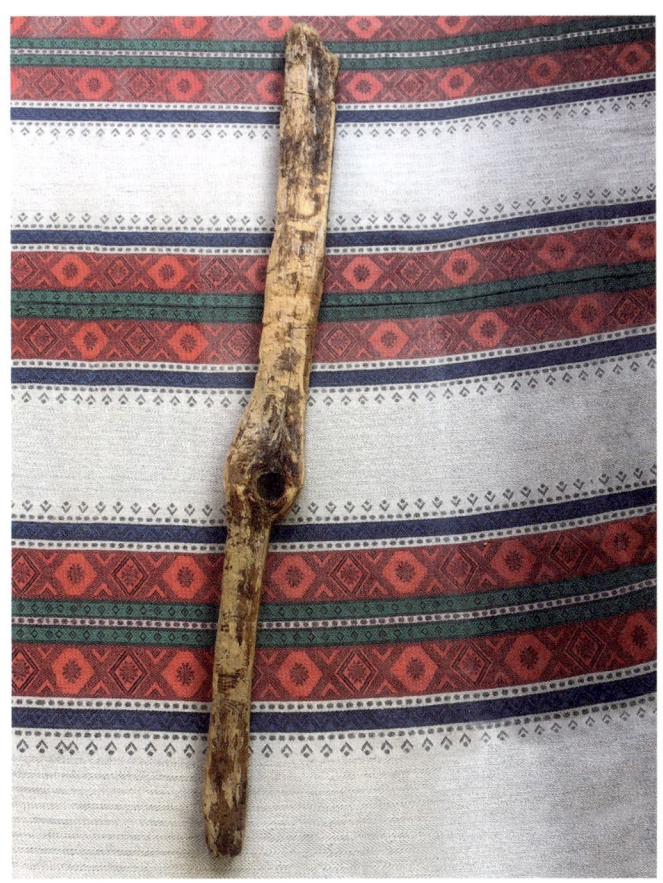

FOUND BY **ILIKO**
LOCATION **MANGLISI, GEORGIA**
CLASS **SWORD**

Magnificent sword from ancient forest,
with an empty place for runestone.

FOUND BY **RICARDO**
LOCATION **INSTITUTE OF
BIOSCIENCES, USP,
SÃO PAULO, BRAZIL**
CLASS **WAND**

This is a wand used only by the best druids of the spore circle. It is made of wood and fungi, and amplifies magic related to fungi.

FOUND BY **ANNKIN**
LOCATION **FÄRJENÄS,
GOTHENBURG, SWEDEN**
CLASS **ARIFACT**

This stick just washed up on the harbor shore with its magical portholes to this other dimension. The glass pieces are from the same Loot Location and fit right in without any adhesive.

FOUND BY **JAAKKO**
LOCATION **SOTKAMO, FINLAND**
CLASS **NATTY**

This full-bodied stick has earthy tones. It was located on a site where a harvester had chopped down old trees, so the expression may be a remnant of that destruction.

FOUND BY **HAIRULD**
LOCATION **SARAWAK,
MALAYSIA**
CLASS **ARTIFACT**

Mirror to see future.

FOUND BY **AARON PYNE THE ELVEN WIZARD**
LOCATION **OREGON, UNITED STATES**
CLASS **STAFF**

The Ancient Elven Orb-Staff of Nature's Wrath is a relic of unparalleled beauty and power, crafted eons ago by the high elven sorcerers of the Verdant Forest. This staff is a symbol of the elves' deep connection to nature and their mastery over its forces. Some whisper that the final essence of the forest was imbued into this staff as the forest had been nearly destroyed by greedy outsiders.

FOUND BY **GRANT**
LOCATION **RICHFIELD, OHIO, UNITED STATES**
CLASS **ARTIFACT**

This appears to be a throat protector that was formerly affixed to Sauron's helm *or* it could be the top half of Saruman's wizard staff. Such an invaluable source for sorcery and inspiration whilst seeking out wonders of the woods.

FOUND BY **JULIUS**
LOCATION **GERMANY**
CLASS **ANIMAL**

We found it while playing at the lake. It looks like a skull with big horns, but unfortunately, one horn is bigger than the other. It has no moss or anything growing on it. It's a bit rough on some places, but the rest of it is pretty smooth.

FOUND BY **HANKO**
LOCATION **KEI MOUTH, SOUTH AFRICA**
CLASS **ANIMAL**

I was walking happily along and almost tripped over what appeared to be a horse's severed head lying on the beach. At first I screamed in terror, as I thought the Mafia was sending me a message. Fortunately, on closer inspection, I realized it was just a stick.

This stick almost looks like an elephant head found at the farm.

FOUND BY **JAKUB**
LOCATION **PORĘBA, POLAND**
CLASS **POLEARM**

This is a double-handed axe. It is a legendary artifact, because it was one of the fragments left from a tree exploded by a lightning strike. We found it on a hike and thought it was cool. We put it by a tree a year ago and forgot about it. Then, a week ago we were on a hike in the same place, and the axe was still in the same place, untouched.

FOUND BY **DANIEL**
LOCATION **DEVIL'S DYKE,
SUSSEX, ENGLAND**
CLASS **POLEARM**

Over-12-foot-tall scythe!!

FOUND BY **VÁCLAV**
LOCATION **CZECH REPUBLIC**
CLASS **POLEARM**

It is super cool stick that looks like a scythe; it also reminds me of the weapon you can buy in *Shadow Fight 2*.

FOUND BY **KENNETH**
LOCATION **HUNTINGTON BEACH,
CALIFORNIA, UNITED STATES**
CLASS **POLEARM**

We were just hanging out at the
beach and found this monster of a
stick that resembles a scythe, and
we took a picture in the moonlight.
(No trees or anything around, so
no clue how it ended up there.)

FOUND BY **PAUL** · LOCATION **CIUCAŞ MOUNTAINS, ROMANIA** · CLASS **SWORD**

It's a perfect pocket knife. Not too big, not too small.

Cool mini scythe.

FOUND BY **CURTIS**
LOCATION **AUSTRALIA**
CLASS **ARTIFACT**

Black plague witch
doctor medicine stick.

FOUND BY **ENIS**
LOCATION **VALBONA VALLEY,
ALBANIA**
CLASS **POLEARM**

The best of course.

This is a little mushroom stick I found in the foothills of Himalayas in India. I imagine forest fairies using it to protect themselves from the snow.

FOUND BY TEO
LOCATION NEW ZEALAND
CLASS POLEARM

It's the Flamingo Axe Stick. First I thought it was a bone, but as soon as I grabbed it, I knew it was the coolest wooden axe I ever had. The blade looks like a flamingo, too, which is a pretty cool design feature. I found this one near Nelson on the south island of New Zealand, and it should be there to this day.

FOUND BY ALEXANDRU
LOCATION ROMANIA
CLASS POLEARM

This piece is an Ancient Phoenix War Axe. Its blade was forged into the shape of a Phoenix Bird's head. It is sturdy and effective in combat. Its size and weight makes it an incredible weapon for close combat. The shape of the blade has 3 functions. 1st is to slash and pierce enemy armor, 2nd is to intimidate enemies, and 3rd is to encourage warriors to fight, giving them the belief that even if they fall in combat, while using this weapon, they will be brought back to life just like a Phoenix Bird.

FOUND BY **ALMANTAS**
LOCATION **GIRELĖS PAŽINTINIS TAKAS
[GROVE SIGHTSEEING TRAIL],
KAIŠIADORYS, LITHUANIA**
CLASS **BLUDGEON**

The Serpent Axe, poison and melee type,
one-handed weapon of destruction.

FOUND BY **TREVOR**
LOCATION **NEW JERSEY, UNITED STATES**
CLASS **BLUDGEON**

I pulled this stick out of the mud when I
was 12. I am now 42, and still think it's bad
azz. It has a perfect molded handle to fit
a man-size hand. Its weight distribution
is perfect! It's a gnarly hard as hell piece
of wood. It is begging for things to be
smashed with it. I am grabbing this in a
zombie apocalypse.

FOUND BY **YAZAN**
LOCATION **AL-TAFILA, JORDAN**
CLASS **ARTILLERY**

It's big and looks like
a giant boomerang.

FOUND BY **ALEX AND JOE**
LOCATION **ALUM BAY, ISLE OF WIGHT, UK**
CLASS **BLUDGEON**

While walking along the beach at Alum Bay on the Isle of Wight, my brother (Joe) and I found this hulking piece of driftwood lying in the sand. As I pulled it out from the sandy depths, I discovered the stick was shaped like a gigantic hammer.

FOUND BY **LUKE AND KIMMIE**
LOCATION **SEATTLE,
WASHINGTON, UNITED STATES**
CLASS **NATTY**

Stick Nation rocks.

FOUND BY **JOVARAS**
LOCATION **BALTIEJI LAKAJAI
(LAKE LAKAJAI),
MOLĖTAI DISTRICT, LITHUANIA**
CLASS **BLUDGEON**

It's a two-handed battle mace which is wielded only by the greatest of warriors.

Strength: 70 · Dexterity: 15
Intellect: 10 · Encumbrance: 15.6

Special skill: Stomp the mace into the ground to stun nearby enemies in a 15 m radius.

FOUND BY **PAUL**
LOCATION **WINNIPEG,
MANITOBA, CANADA**
CLASS **BLUDGEON**

It's a giant club-looking stick.
It would be good for clubbing things.

FOUND BY **TIM**
LOCATION **SANTA CLAUS BEACH,
CALIFORNIA, UNITED STATES**
CLASS **BLUDGEON**

Yo Stick Nation!
Check this mondo beach stick.

FOUND BY **ANDREI**
LOCATION **RIO DE JANEIRO, BRAZIL**
CLASS **BLUDGEON**

This is a mystical hammer used a long time ago by a little-known magician from the Brazilian Atlantic forest. Its power is not physical, but magical, and it can set off powerful waves of impact and transfiguration.

FOUND BY **IGOR**
LOCATION **ZARASAI, LITHUANIA**
CLASS **BLUDGEON**

It's a big wooden hammer which was created by forest gods to protect the forests from evil. Anyone who's found that stick is nominated as a guardian of the forest.

FOUND BY **EREN**
LOCATION **TÜRKIYE**
CLASS **BLUDGEON**

This stick is a legendary power hammer stick. It weighs approximately a few kilos and is seriously extremely difficult to lift!

FOUND BY **AASHISH**
LOCATION **INDIA**
CLASS **SWORD**

British longsword—Excalibur.

FOUND BY **CHANDAN**
LOCATION **INDIA**
CLASS **SWORD**

The Black Knife scales primarily
with Faith and Dexterity and
is a good Weapon for dealing
additional Holy Damage and
for its Unique Skill, Blade of
Death, that allows the user to
fire an additional projectile.

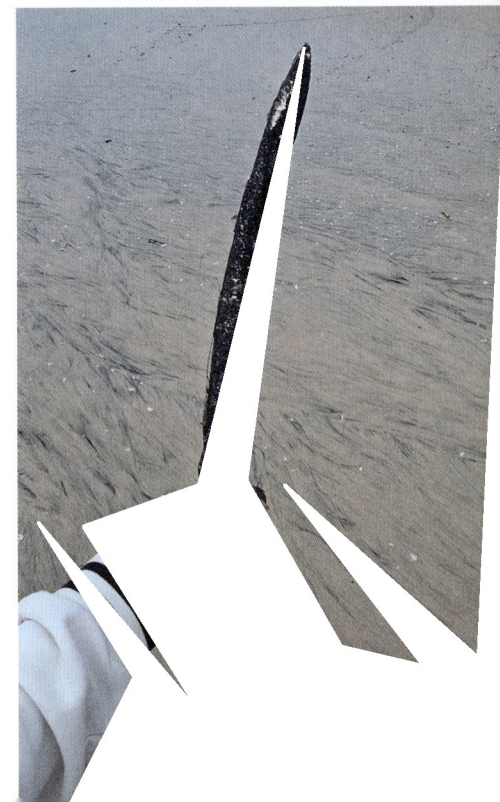

FOUND BY **ARTHUR**
LOCATION **SALAR DE UYUNI, BOLIVIA**
CLASS **SWORD**

It's a dagger or a short sword that has to be a cactus's root since there are no trees on the island in the middle of the Salar. It takes its power from the salt of the Salar.

FOUND BY **CHRISTIAN**
LOCATION **INNSBRUCK, AUSTRIA**
CLASS **SWORD**

I found this mythical sword while hiking on the Nordkette near Innsbruck. It is really well balanced and feels great. Although I can't prove to be the lawful ruler of Tyrol now, I definitely won a really cool stick on that day.

FOUND BY **OLIVER**
LOCATION **SWITZERLAND**
CLASS **SWORD**

Yo, I found this stick when I was like 7 years old. We used to play in the woods and build our own base. When I found it, I knew it was a SWORD!

FOUND BY **NICOLAJ**
LOCATION **NORWAY**
CLASS **SWORD**

I went to visit my girlfriend in
Norway. While she was working,
I went for a walk in the woods
nearby and came across this stick.
I, of course, picked up the stick
and was instantly transported to
another realm.

FOUND BY **BRETT**
LOCATION **LAKE ALOHA,
CALIFORNIA, UNITED STATES**
CLASS **SWORD**

Found this stick near a beautiful
channel in Lake Aloha while on
an overnight backpacking trip.
Is giving *Zelda/Final Fantasy*.

FOUND BY **COLE**
LOCATION **LOTHLÓRIEN FOREST, NEW ZEALAND**
CLASS **SWORD**

Was taking a walk in New Zealand, near Glenorchy, and came across the coolest stick of all time.

FOUND BY **RHANNA**
LOCATION **ILHA DO MEL (HONEY ISLAND), PARANÁ, BRAZIL**
CLASS **POLEARM**

It is a bone magic stick, found on the beach of a protected island in the south of Brazil. The curve with some spikes reminds me of the human spinal column.

FOUND BY **WALDT**
LOCATION **THE CÉVENNES, FRANCE**
CLASS **NATTY**

I found a huuuge stick in the south of France today. I named it Big Little Boy. Despite his size, he was OK to walk with and carry. The stick gives a real energy when you walk and you shake it. The weight of the stick feels like waves in the whole body. I had a real vibe with it.

FOUND BY **SOFIA**
LOCATION **KOH LIPE, THAILAND**
CLASS **STAFF**

Large beach stick. Smooth, similar to a two-pronged trident. Tandem wielding. Well balanced. Potential use as battering ram or land beacon. Unsure whether originated from ocean or future driftwood.

FOUND BY **LUCA AND MICHELE**
LOCATION **SAN MENAIO, APULIA, ITALY**
CLASS **ARTILLERY**

Three huge slings used by giants in the war of Gargano in Apulia!

FOUND BY **PRISHITA** • LOCATION **OOTY, INDIA**
CLASS **SWORD, POLEARM, AND ARTILLERY**

Me and my friends had a big forest search to find sticks that match our personalities—and we did find our sticks! One of them is a boomerang; one of them is a javelin; and one of them is a sword.

FOUND BY **LEONARDO AND FRIENDS**
LOCATION **LAGO DELLA NINFA, ITALY**
CLASS **STASH**

We challenged each other to find the best
sticks around, and this is our result!

ACKNOWLEDGMENTS

First, I want to thank Steve Kurutz and *The New York Times*. Your article captured the spirit of Official Stick Reviews and brought our niche community into the spotlight.

Thank you to our editor, Molly Birnbaum, and the team at Ten Speed Press for seeing our potential and actually publishing a book about sticks.

Thank you to my brother, Jackson. Your creative eye and photography elevated this book.

Thank you to the rest of my family. You all are the best support system.

Thank you to my father for always believing I could fly. Thank you to my mother for the constant support and unconditional love.

To my wife and creator of the Tennison Curve Scale, Cheyenne. You are my favorite person alive. You film me talking about sticks and still love me. I love you.

And lastly, thank you to every member of Stick Nation. Stick Nation is all of us. Always stick together.

—Boone

Shout out to Sierra, all my friends, and everyone in Stick Nation who made this book a possibility.

Stick Nation forever.

—Logan

ABOUT THE AUTHORS

Boone Hogg and Logan Jugler are the creators of @officialstickreviews, the highly popular online community. Official Stick Reviews has connected millions of people from around the world who love sticks and nature. Often called the "most wholesome place on the internet," Official Stick Reviews provides a space for people from all walks of life to share their stick treasures and connect through the simplicity of being human.

Hogg is based in Utah and spends his time with his wife, family, and stick-loving dog, Mochi. Jugler is based in California and likes to spend his time adventuring with his girlfriend.

TEN SPEED PRESS
An imprint of the Crown Publishing Group
A division of Penguin Random House LLC
1745 Broadway
New York, NY 10019
tenspeed.com
penguinrandomhouse.com

Typefaces: TypeType's TT Norms and Resistenza's
Dolce Caffe

Library of Congress Cataloging-in-Publication
Data is on file with the publisher.

Hardcover ISBN: 978-0-593-83752-8
Ebook ISBN: 978-0-593-83753-5

Acquiring editor: Molly Birnbaum
Production editors: Ashley Pierce and Bridget Sweet
Editorial assistant: Kausaur Fahimuddin
Art director and designer: Kelly Booth
Production designers: Mari Gill and Claudia Sanchez
Production manager: Dan Myers | Prepress color
manager and retoucher: Claudia Sanchez
Copyeditor: Kristi Hein | Proofreaders: Mark
Burstein and Sasha Tropp
Publicist: David Hawk | Marketer: Monica Stanton

Manufactured in China

10 9 8 7 6 5 4 3 2 1

First Edition

Cover photograph by Jackson Hogg
Back cover photograph by Gary Hogg

The authorized representative in the EU for
product safety and compliance is Penguin
Random House Ireland, Morrison Chambers,
32 Nassau Street, Dublin D02 YH68, Ireland,
https://eu-contact.penguin.ie.

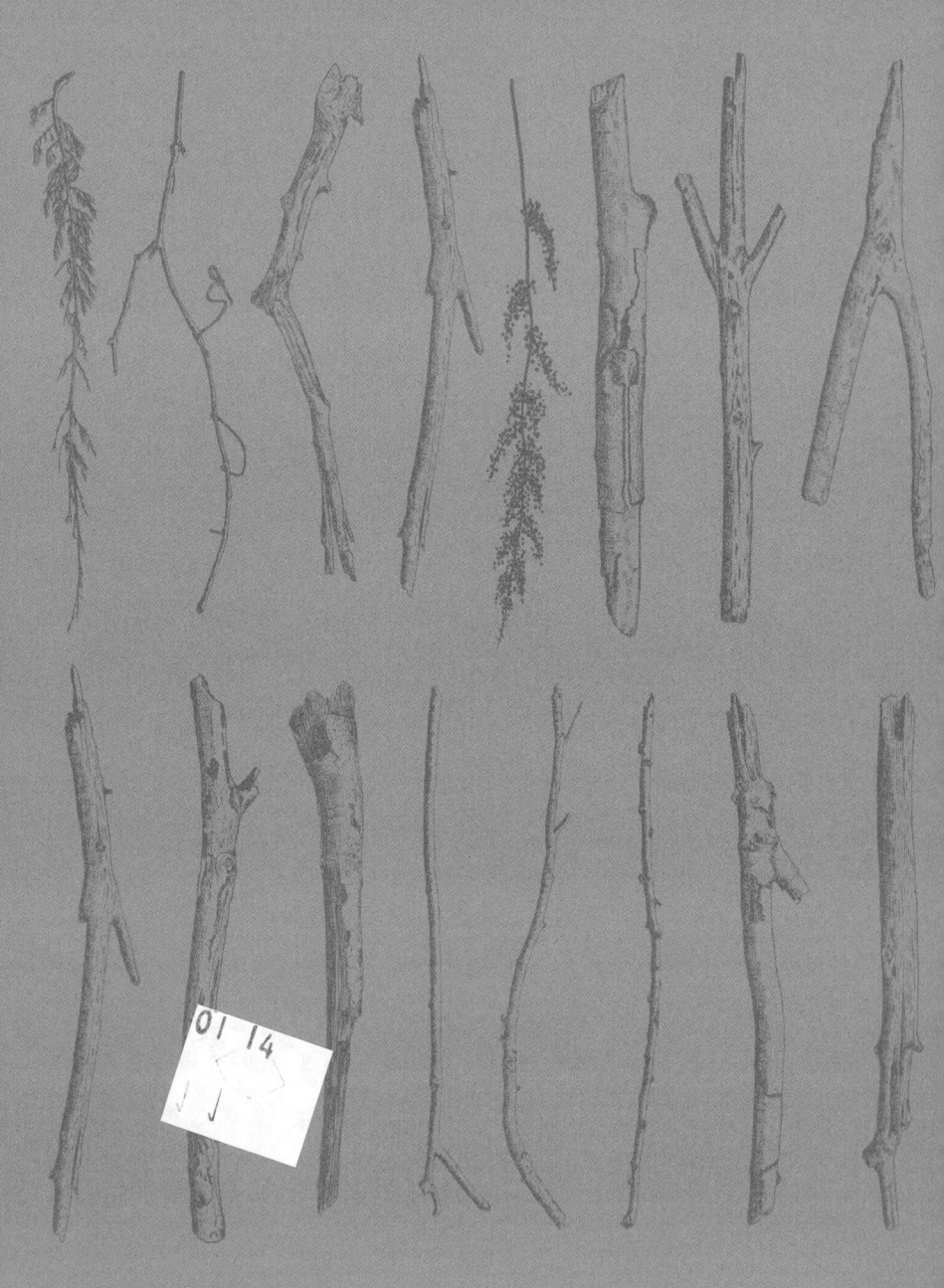